The Stubborn Princess

T0359655

Written by Jenny Feely

Illustrated by Ian Forss

Flying Start
to Literacy®

Contents

Chapter 1

Gifts for a princess

When Princess Nadia was born, the lords and ladies came from all over the kingdom to celebrate. The King held the baby up for all to see.

"She will be kind," said one lady.

"She will be wise," said a lord.

And so it went. One by one the lords and
ladies came forward to greet Princess Nadia
and give their gifts and their good wishes.

The King and Queen stood next to the baby's
cradle, smiling happily. Then the doors flew
open and in strode a tall woman dressed
all in black.

"I see you have forgotten to invite me,"
said Vani, with a sneer. "Not to worry.
I have something for the baby anyway."

She strode up to Princess Nadia and in a loud
voice cried, "She will be stubborn!"

And with that, she turned and disappeared
before anyone could stop her.

The King and Queen turned pale. Who had
ever heard of a stubborn princess?

Anisha, a wise woman respected by all in the kingdom, stepped forward.

"Stubbornness and persistence are very alike," she said. "It's not a bad thing to be persistent. Perhaps a stubborn princess is just what this kingdom needs."

Chapter 2

A royal pet

As Princess Nadia grew, she seemed like any other princess and people forgot the words of both Vani and Anisha.

Then Princess Nadia turned eight and everything changed.

"I want a pet," she said.

"How sweet," said the Queen. "How about a soft, furry kitten?"

"No!" said the princess. "I want a spider – a big, hairy spider."

"Ridiculous!" said the Queen.

"Preposterous!" said the King. "Princesses do not have spiders for pets."

But Princess Nadia persisted. Every day she asked for a pet spider. She did not give up.

"She is so stubborn," said the King.

"Whatever will we do?" said the Queen. "She just won't give up."

"I have an idea," said the King. "Perhaps once she sees how terrifying such a pet is, she will change her mind."

So the King and Queen decided to send Princess Nadia to Anisha's cottage. Anisha kept a huge collection of dangerous animals which she studied.

"Nadia, you are going to help Anisha with her animals," said the King. "That way, you can see whether you really do like dangerous animals."

"Oh, I will!" said Princess Nadia, running off toward Anisha's cottage excitedly.

The first animal Anisha showed Nadia was the newest in her collection – the biggest, hairiest spider that had ever been seen.

"He's beautiful!" said Princess Nadia.

Anisha taught Princess Nadia how to look after the spider and how to catch insects for him to eat. And most importantly, she taught her how to stay away from the spider's fearsome, long fangs.

"This is a dangerous animal with deadly venom in those fangs," said Anisha.

But Nadia wasn't scared at all. "I know," she said. "That's why I love him. Dangerous animals are so interesting."

The spider was only one of Anisha's huge collection of animals that Nadia would grow to love. As time went on, Princess Nadia was introduced to more and more deadly and dangerous pets. And she loved them all.

Nadia adored the death stalker scorpion and thought that the death adder was entrancing. In her opinion, the poison arrow frogs were the cutest things she had ever seen.

Anisha had a huge lake by her cottage filled with salty seawater to keep her blue-ringed octopuses safe and happy.

Nadia loved helping Anisha look after her animals. But most of all, she loved learning about their deadly and dangerous ways. One day she planned to have a collection of her very own.

Then Prince Raja was born and everything changed.

Chapter 3

Gifts for a prince

Once again the lords and ladies came from all over the kingdom to give their gifts and good wishes.

"He will be handsome," said one lord.

"He will be brave," said a lady.

And so it went. Then suddenly the doors flew open and in strode Vani once more.

"You'll be sorry you didn't check your invitation list," she said to the King and Queen. "It seems you have forgotten me again!"

She stooped over the baby. "He will be fearless!" she boomed, laughing wickedly.

Then before anyone could stop her she was gone.

"Well," said the King. "That's a relief. He was already blessed with bravery anyway. Princes are meant to be brave and fearless."

But Anisha shook her head. "I'm not so sure that being brave and fearless are the same thing," she said.

As Prince Raja grew, everyone could see that he was both brave and fearless. He would climb the highest trees and swim across the deepest rivers without a second thought. He laughed when he saw a charging bull. He was not afraid of anything.

One day Prince Raja disappeared. The King and the Queen had the castle searched from top to bottom. No one could find him.

Princess Nadia was at Anisha's cottage, observing the poison arrow frogs, when she heard her brother's giggle coming from the other room.

"Oh, no," she cried to Anisha. "Raja must have followed me here!"

Nadia and Anisha reached the doorway just in time to see Raja removing the lid to the spider's tank and reaching inside.

"Stop!" cried Anisha as she pulled Prince Raja away from the tank. "That spider is deadly and dangerous. You should be very afraid of putting your hand in there!"

"I'm not afraid of spiders," laughed Raja. "I'm not afraid of anything."

Chapter 4

No more pets!

When the King and Queen found out that Raja was almost bitten by a spider, they were shocked and upset.

"This is too much," said the Queen. "Nadia must learn that those animals are dangerous. We must protect both of our children from them!"

"I agree," said the King. "Those animals are deadly. Our children must never go to Anisha's cottage ever again."

"No!" cried Princess Nadia. "There is so much I can learn from the animals. They may be dangerous, but they are useful too."

"How can they be useful?" asked the King.

Nadia's face fell. "I don't know yet," she said. "But I am sure I can find out if you will just let me study them."

But the King and Queen would not change their minds.

Two knights were ordered to watch over Prince Raja and keep him safe. It was a difficult job, but they did it well. Another knight had to make sure that Princess Nadia did not go to Anisha's cottage.

But one night, Nadia was so persistent in her attempts to escape that the knight got no sleep at all. The next day when he fell asleep, exhausted, Princess Nadia snuck past him and ran to Anisha's cottage to visit her beloved pets.

"Princess Nadia," said Anisha, surprised. "You shouldn't be here. But since you are, I have something exciting to show you!"

Anisha held up a small bottle.

"Inside this bottle is a potion made from venom," she said. "It can save people's lives if they are bitten by a deadly animal."

Nadia rushed back to the castle to tell the King and Queen. Surely her parents would allow her to keep helping Anisha once they knew how useful the animals were!

Chapter 5

A surprise gift

Princess Nadia burst into the throne room, but only Raja was there. He had found a large gift behind the King's throne. His name was written on the tag and it was signed "From Vani".

"Who's Vani?" he said, as he ripped off the paper and opened the box.

"Don't open it," said Princess Nadia. "There might be something dangerous inside."

"So what?" said Prince Raja. "I'm not afraid of anything."

And he reached into the box before anyone could stop him.

"Ow! Ow! Ow!" he cried, clutching his hand.

A knight ran over and grabbed the box.
Out slithered a very big, very angry snake.
Prince Raja began to shiver and shake.
Then he collapsed on the floor.

The King and the Queen rushed into the
throne room.

"That's the most deadly snake in the
kingdom!" cried the Queen.

"Nothing can save him now," said the King.

"I can," said Princess Nadia, and she rushed
out of the throne room. "I have just the
thing. I only hope I have enough time."

When Nadia returned, Raja's face was grey.

"This potion will save someone who has been bitten by a snake!" said Princess Nadia, holding up a small bottle.

"What's it made from?" asked the Queen.

"From snake venom," said Princess Nadia.

"Ridiculous!" said the King.

"Preposterous," said the Queen. "You can't cure someone by giving them more venom."

Nadia ran to Raja and carefully opened the bottle.

"You will poison him with that!" said the King.

"No, I won't," said Nadia.

"You don't know that it will work," said the Queen.

"Yes, I do," said Nadia stubbornly, and before anyone could stop her, she gave Raja the potion.

Chapter 6

Ever after

Everyone held their breath and waited. Slowly, the colour crept back into Raja's face.

"It's working," said the King.

"You've saved him," said the Queen.

From that day on things changed once more in the kingdom. Prince Raja had at last learned the difference between being brave and being fearless, and now he was much more careful.

Princess Nadia was allowed to help Anisha with her pets again. She continued to study them. It wasn't easy but she did not give up. The amazing discoveries she made with Anisha helped the kingdom in many ways. The King and Queen were very proud of Nadia.

"I suppose a stubborn princess is just what we needed," said the King.

A note from the author

In this story I wanted to create a female character who was strong and intelligent – a girl who wasn't afraid to try new things and would persist when she knew that she was right.

I also wanted to explore how persistence can become stubbornness and how fearlessness can become foolishness.

As I thought about how this book would link to *Deadly Venom: Killer or Cure?*, it seemed logical to have Princess Nadia involved in finding a cure to save people bitten by venomous animals.